To _____

From _____

....

....

....

(For more prayer helps, go to www.WordWay.org)

Grown-ups need to talk to God every day, too!

Prayers for Our Lives: 95 Lifelines to God for Everyday Circumstances (WordWay 2016).

by Mel Lawrenz

"Mel writes with disarming honesty, and each prayer is like a cry of the heart. Here child-like simplicity meets sage-like wisdom, all of it spoken so intimately that living breath still fills each word. Lifelines indeed."

—MARK BUCHANAN, author, pastor, and professor

www.PrayersForOurLives.org

www.PrayersForOurLives.org

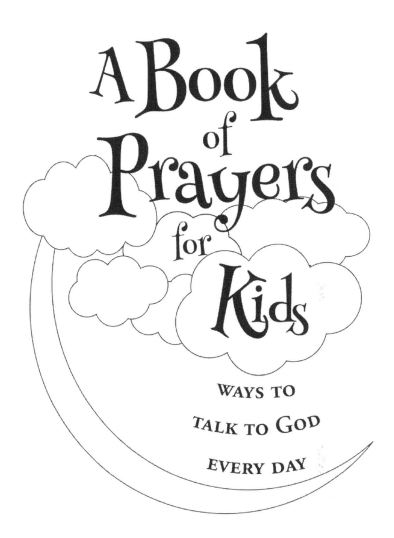

A Book of Prayers for Kids

of

WAYS TO

TALK TO GOD

EVERY DAY

— MEL LAWRENZ —

WORDWAY
WWW.WORDWAY.ORG

Eva Helen Lawrenz (1987-2017) had a passion for truth, literature, and the world. "Eva" means life (Hebrew), and "Helen" means light (Greek). Life And Light Books are dedicated to her memory and for the purpose of glorifying God through the ministry of the written word.
MORE: LifeAndLightBooks.org

CONTENTS

A Word to Young Readers

I'm sure you know this already, but you can pray to God anytime, anywhere you wish. Prayer can be out-loud words, or silent words, reading a prayer that was written by someone else, or reading a prayer in the Bible. Sometimes we need help knowing what to pray. That is why Jesus' disciples said to Jesus one day: "Teach us to pray."

It is really important to pray. Even if it is a single sentence here and there throughout the day. Praying is a way to stay connected to God. That is what we need when we're having a good day, and when we're having a very bad day. God has told us that he wants us to talk to him. So praying makes God glad. There are some times in life when we don't know what to do to make a situation better. Well, we can pray. Maybe the situation will get better, or maybe things will be better just because we talked to God. Praying helps us to be brave, to lessen our worries, to help other people. Praying will help us make better decisions, get along better with our families, and keep faithful to God.

This book is for you. Mark it up. Make notes in the margins. Write your own prayers. Use your colored pencils or pens to write your responses, your thoughts, or to sketch or color or doodle.

This is *not* a book to store on a bookshelf. Instead, leave it on your bed stand, keep it in your family room, bring it to the dining table, put it in your backpack when you go to school, take it with you when you travel. Try different prayers. Memorize a few.

Try using it every day for a few weeks, and see how things change for you. You do not need to read this page by page.

Use the table of contents or thumb through the book to find prayers that you need for each day.

Here's the best part, friends. God loves us all so much, and he loves it when you talk to him. And then, God shows his heart to us.

I don't know you personally, but I know that God has good things in store for your life. Just stay connected to God!

Mel Lawrenz

P.S. Do you know why we often say "Amen" at the end of praying? In the Bible "Amen" means "this is true!" So when we say "Amen" it is like saying: I really mean this! I believe this is true!

P.P.S. Our prayers are strong when they are based on the truths of the Bible. So you will see a Bible verse or passage with every prayer in this book. Think carefully about them.

A Word for the Adult Who Gave This Book

You may be a parent, grandparent, aunt or uncle, Sunday school teacher, family friend, or next door neighbor. For some reason you chose to get this book and to gift it to someone you know. Your generosity honors God.

The purpose for this book of prayers for kids is simple: to give kids the means to stay connected to God. (It is aimed at kids aged 7 to 12, approximately. But kids may start younger or go older.)

I remember when my daughter and son were just kids, and how I knew that there was nothing more important I could do than to help them have their own relationship with God. I emphasize "their own relationship" because I knew I had to reject the temptation to think I could control them in what they believe and what they think about and feel about God. This, of course, can never result in true faith.

I believed then and I believe now that adults can help kids use or memorize set prayers, and that this is very beneficial. This is not a substitute for them praying spontaneously, in their own words. Using written prayers is a way of learning how to pray. Written prayers may show that it is okay to say anything to God, and that we should be honest and forthcoming. When Jesus' disciples said, "teach us to pray," he did not do a lecture on methods of prayer. Jesus just gave them a model prayer, which we know as the Lord's Prayer.

As you can see from the table of contents, this book contains prayers for daily patterns, for specific situations, for family and friends, for special occasions, etc. If you familiarize yourself with these, you may be able to remind your young friend at times when he or she needs to connect with God.

You may be able to teach your young friend or child by talking through the words of the prayers as you use them. For instance, "A Prayer to Start the Day" includes phrases about thoughts, words, and actions, a classic way of talking about all of life. If there is a new word in a prayer here and there, that is a chance for kids to add new ideas to their minds and vocabularies.

Some people ask: Do prayers need to be directed toward God the Father, or Jesus, or the Holy Spirit? The Bible has examples of each, and mostly prayers to "God" or the "Lord," which means praying to all of God—Father, Son, and Holy Spirit. God allows us to speak in any of these ways.

What about praying "in Jesus' name"? Sometimes we use these words at the end of a prayer, but not as a required magic phrase. All praying done believing in Jesus as our mediator and with his authority is praying "in his name." So you will see a variety of prayer endings in these prayers.

I'm encouraging kids *not* to keep this book on a bookshelf, but to keep it in their backpacks, on their night stands, in the family room, at the dinner table, etc. This collection of prayers is more like foods in your pantry for daily access than medicines locked away in a medicine chest for emergency needs.

Thank you for loving the young friend you are giving this to. And lest you feel left out, check out the book of prayers for adults: *Prayers for Our Lives: 95 Lifelines to God for Everyday Circumstances* at www.PrayersForOurLives.org.

Mel Lawrenz

- A Book of Prayers for Kids -

Part 1

Prayers
for
Every Day

A Mealtime Prayer

Thank you, Lord, for this food we share,

thank you, Lord, that we know you care.

Make my body strong for you,

Keep my heart pure and true.

Amen.

God's Word says...

"Therefore I tell you, do not worry about your life, what you will eat or drink; or about your body, what you will wear. Is not life more than food, and the body more than clothes? Look at the birds of the air; they do not sow or reap or store away in barns, and yet your heavenly Father feeds them. Are you not much more valuable than they? Can any one of you by worrying add a single hour to your life?"

Matthew 6:25

A Prayer to Start the Day

Thank you, Lord, for this brand-new day.

Keep me safe, keep me strong, I pray.

Guide my actions,

shape my thoughts,

tell me what to say.

Help me to follow your good, pure way. Amen.

God's Word says...

"And whatever you do... do it all in the name of the Lord Jesus, giving thanks to God the Father through him."

Colossians 3:17

Think about this: What can you do today that will be good, and what are things that might waste your time?

A Prayer to End the Day

Lord, the day is now over and I will soon go to

sleep. You were with me through this day, as you will

be tomorrow. Thank you for your blessings.

I'm sorry for mistakes I made. I rest in your

forgiveness, and I ask for your help tomorrow. I pray

for a good night's sleep. And I pray that tomorrow I

can make a new beginning, walking with you

wherever I go. Amen.

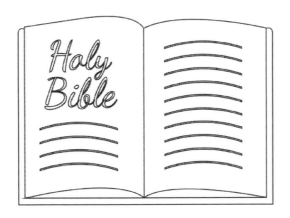

God's Word says...

"In peace I will lie down and sleep,

for you alone, Lord,

make me dwell in safety."

Psalm 4:8

Before You Read the Bible

Lord, open my eyes so that I can understand

what you are saying in the Bible.

I know I will have questions,

so give me patience to find your answers.

Give me faith to trust what I read,

and give me courage to obey.

Amen.

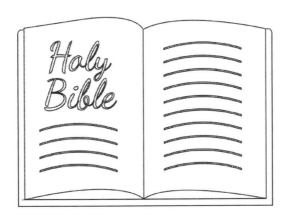

God's Word says...

"All Scripture is God-breathed and is useful for teaching, rebuking, correcting and training in righteousness, so that the servant of God may be thoroughly equipped for every good work."

2 Timothy 3:16-17

(Can you think of something to draw or color here?)

Part 2

Prayers
for
Needy Times

(You may want to write your own thoughts and prayers for these.)

When You Are Afraid

Dear God,

I really need you now because I am afraid.

I know you are greater than anyone else.

I know you are bigger than anything I face.

I know you are good when things are bad.

I know you are everywhere.

I know you love me.

I know things can change.

Help me to wait in the safety of your care.

In Jesus' name, Amen.

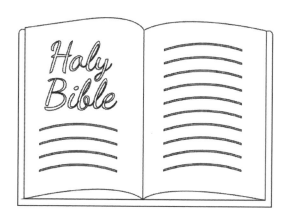

God's Word Says...

"The Lord is my light and my salvation—
whom shall I fear?
The Lord is the stronghold of my life—
of whom shall I be afraid?"

Psalm 27:1

When You Are Sad

Dear Lord,

Today I am sad. I do not like this.

You know why I am sad,

and I am glad that you do.

That lets me know I am not alone.

Show me if there is something I should do.

Tell me if there is something I should say.

I know I will not always feel this way.

I trust you. In Jesus' name, Amen.

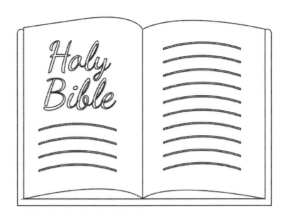

God's Word says...

"Praise be to the God and Father of our Lord Jesus Christ, the Father of compassion and the God of all comfort, who comforts us in all our troubles, so that we can comfort those in any trouble with the comfort we ourselves receive from God."

2 Corinthians 1:3-4

When You Are Lonely

Dear God,

I call out to you now

because I am feeling lonely.

I do not like this feeling. I do not want to be

alone. So I need you now, dear God.

I understand that you are with me,

but I need to truly know that in my heart.

People are around me, but I need to know

how I can connect with them.

Show me how to trust, and

how to be careful. Amen.

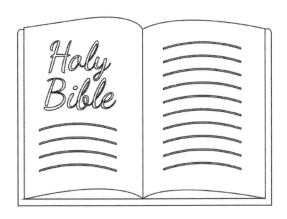

God's Word says...

"As the Father has loved me, so have I loved you. Now remain in my love. If you keep my commands, you will remain in my love, just as I have kept my Father's commands and remain in his love. I have told you this so that my joy may be in you and that your joy may be complete."

John 15:9-11

When You've Lost a Friend

Dear Lord,

I am sad because it seems like I have lost a friend.

I wish this were not so.

Maybe we can be friends again, but maybe not.

I need to know that things will be okay

one way or another.

I know, Lord Jesus, that you are the most

important friend I have.

Please guide me to find others who are your

friends as well. Amen.

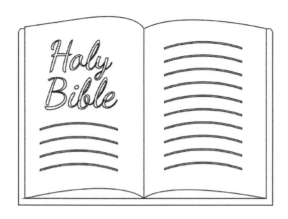

God's Word says...

"I have called you friends, for everything that I learned from my Father I have made known to you."

John 15:15

Think about this: Who are friends who help me and support me? Who should I be careful around because they have hurt me at times?

When You Are Being Bullied

Lord, I really need your help now. I am so mad
and hurt and afraid when I am being bullied. It is
making me feel ashamed in front of others. I need
more strength, Jesus, to stand up for myself. I need
to be smart about how I react. I need protection.
Show me if I should be doing something different.

Lord God, protect me.

Help me to know this is not my fault. Help me
trust that you, dear God, stand for what is right, and
that those who do wrong will not get away with it.

I pray in the name of Jesus, who is Lord of all
things. Amen.

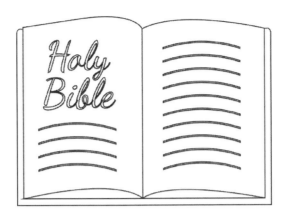

God's Word says...

"Therefore let all the faithful pray to you
while you may be found;
surely the rising of the mighty waters
will not reach them.
You are my hiding place;
you will protect me from trouble
and surround me with songs of deliverance."

Psalm 36:6-7

Sometimes people who bully others have been hurt by someone else. Pray for them.

When You Are Confused

I am very confused right now, dear God.

I do not understand what other people are doing

and why they are saying what they are saying.

Help me to understand.

And if I can't understand right now,

help me to be strong and confident

by holding on to you. Amen.

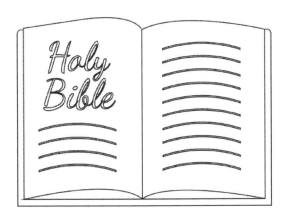

God's Word says...

"Don't worry about anything; instead, pray about everything. Tell God what you need, and thank him for all he has done. Then you will experience God's peace, which exceeds anything we can understand. His peace will guard your hearts and minds as you live in Christ Jesus."

Philippians 4:6-7 (TEV)

When You Have Done Wrong

I have done something wrong, Lord.

I confess it to you.

I am embarrassed and I am sorry.

I am not sure who I should talk to about this, so

please help me figure that out.

When I do talk, help me have the right words.

If I can make things right, give me the courage to

do that. But right now, right here, Lord, I seek to

know your love and forgiveness.

In the name of Jesus, Amen.

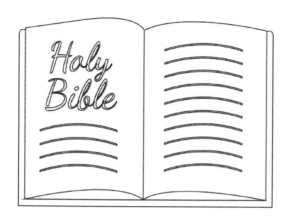

God's Word says...

"If we claim to be without sin, we deceive ourselves and the truth is not in us. If we confess our sins, he is faithful and just and will forgive us our sins and purify us from all unrighteousness."

1 John 1:8-9

When Someone You Love Has Died

Dear God, I am facing a great loss. Someone I care about has died. This is so hard. I don't fully understand this. I am glad that I can trust you where my understanding falls short. I know that you are good, otherwise there would be no goodness in our lives. So help me to trust you today. Please help the others who are sad right now. Help me to show respect toward them. Amen.

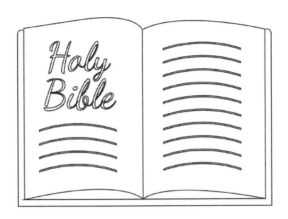

God's Word says...

"When Jesus saw [Mary] weeping, and the Jews who had come along with her also weeping, he was deeply moved in spirit and troubled. 'Where have you laid him?' he asked.

'Come and see, Lord,' they replied.

Jesus wept."

John 11:33-35

When Your Pet Is Ill

Dear God, you are the creator of all things,

including our pets. I know that you love everything

that you have made, and that includes my pet.

I pray for things to get better.

Help us to know what we can do.

Amen.

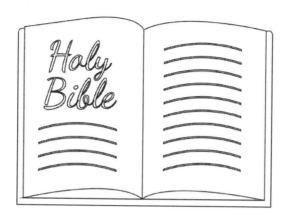

God's Word says...

"Are not five sparrows sold for two pennies? Yet not one of them is forgotten by God."

Luke 12:6

_____

(Draw your favorite animal here.)

When You Have to Say Sorry

Lord, I have done something wrong toward

someone and I know I need to say I'm sorry.

But I am afraid to do that.

Afraid that I will seem weak.

Afraid that they will not accept my apology.

Afraid that I may be wrong.

Help me to be brave and do what is right,

no matter what they say.

In Jesus' name. Amen.

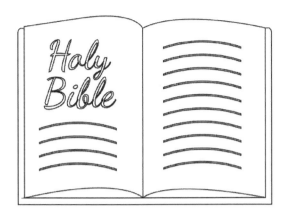

God's Word says...

"Therefore confess your sins to each other and pray for each other so that you may be healed."

James 5:16

When You Are Disappointed

Dear God,

I am disappointed.

Things did not go the way I wanted them to.

I feel like I've lost something important.

It does not seem fair.

I do not want to be a complainer, Lord,

but I know that I can be honest with you.

Help me to focus on my blessings today.

And help me to be patient. I know you are always

working toward what is good, Amen.

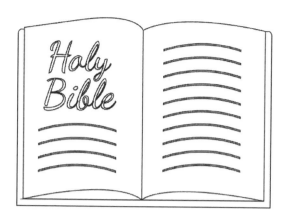

God's Word says...

"The Lord hears his people when they call to him for help.

He rescues them from all their troubles.

The Lord is close to the brokenhearted;

he rescues those whose spirits are crushed."

Psalm 34:17-18

When You Have a Test (or a Tryout)

Dear Lord,

Help me to be confident when I am worried.

Help me to get ready;

help me to do my best;

and help me to accept the results.

Lord, I trust in your love.

I want to keep learning and growing into the

person you want me to be.

In Jesus' name, Amen.

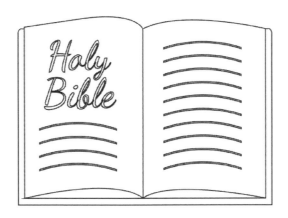

God's Word Says...

"Trust in the Lord with all your heart

and lean not on your own understanding;

in all your ways submit to him,

and he will make your paths straight."

Proverbs 3:5-6

(Can you think of something to draw or color here?)

Part 3

Prayers
of
Praise and
Thanks
to
GOD

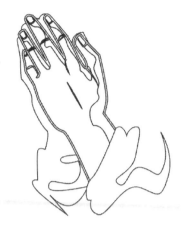

To God Our Father

You are great, our Father in heaven, and you are
good. Great because your power is more than any
evil or good force in the world. Great because you
are everywhere at all times. There is nothing I need
to do for you to be with me, for you are with me at
all times. You are great because you know all things.
You know me when I am awake and when I am
asleep; when I feel great faith and when my faith is
shaky. You know my past and my future. You know
my strengths and my weaknesses. You know what I
truly need. I trust you, my Father. Help me when it is
hard to trust. Amen.

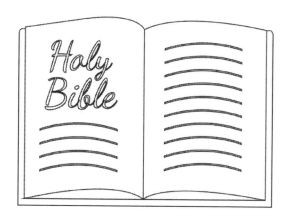

God's Word says...

"Every good and perfect gift is from above, coming down from the Father of the heavenly lights, who does not change like shifting shadows."

James 1:17

To Jesus the Son of God

Lord Jesus, there is no one like you. You are the
Beautiful Savior, the Good Shepherd, the Great
Teacher. You are the Bread sent from heaven, the
Beginning and the End, the Messiah.

You are Lord of lords, King of kings, the Judge
of all things, the beloved Son of God.

You called us your friends. What a friend you are
to us! You have been patient with us, loved us,
forgiven us.

Help me to follow you this day, Lord Jesus. Help
me to see you right there with me.

I love you Jesus. I truly do. Amen.

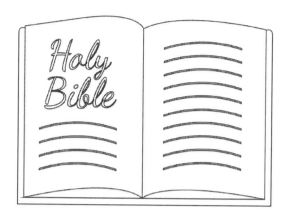

God's Word says...

"I am the good shepherd; I know my sheep and my sheep know me— just as the Father knows me and I know the Father—and I lay down my life for the sheep."

John 10:14-15

To God the Holy Spirit

Holy Spirit,

like a mighty wind, you are invisible but powerful.

I know you must be doing your work among us,

otherwise good things would not happen.

Please put in my mind good thoughts that come

from you. Please help me to know the right thing to

do and say throughout the day. Help me to keep in

step with where you are leading me. Amen.

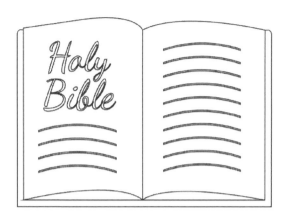

God's Word says...

"And I will ask the Father, and he will give you another advocate to help you and be with you forever the Spirit of truth. The world cannot accept him, because it neither sees him nor knows him. But you know him, for he lives with you and will be in you."

John 14:16-17

Prayer for Faith

Dear Lord, I believe in you,

but I need more faith right now.

My confidence is shaky these days.

But I know I need you.

I want to love you today, and for all times.

Help me to be faithful.

In Jesus' name, Amen.

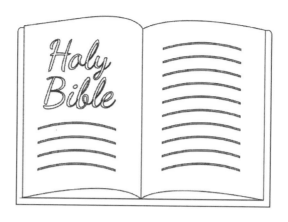

God's Word says...

"Now faith is confidence in what we hope for and assurance about what we do not see."

Hebrews 11:1

Prayer for Hope

I do not know what will happen tomorrow, and

in the months to come, dear God, but you do.

You have promised that you will always be with

us, and will never abandon us.

Help me to trust.

You are good in every way.

You are great in every way.

I know there are good things ahead.

In the name of Jesus, Amen.

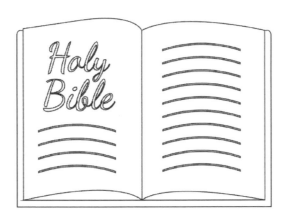

God's Word Says...

"Even youths grow tired and weary,

and young men stumble and fall;

but those who hope in the Lord

will renew their strength.

They will soar on wings like eagles;

they will run and not grow weary,

they will walk and not be faint."

Isaiah 40:30-31

Prayer for Love

Lord, I know how good it is when I know I am
loved by you and by my family and friends.
But I know that many people have little love in
their hearts. I know some loving people seem to
have a change of heart.
Help me to trust in your love that
never shrinks and never changes.
Help me to be a person of love.
Help me to love people who love me,
and even people who seem to dislike me.
I praise you because your love never goes away.
Amen.

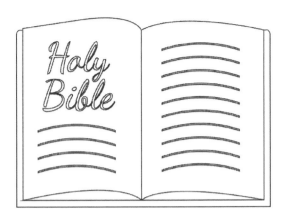

God's Word says...

"Love is patient, love is kind. It does not envy, it does not boast, it is not proud. It does not dishonor others, it is not self-seeking, it is not easily angered, it keeps no record of wrongs. Love does not delight in evil but rejoices with the truth. It always protects, always trusts, always hopes, always perseveres."

1 Corinthians 13:4-7

When You Are Glad

Dear God, today is a very good day.

Thank you for your many blessings.

Thank you for your great love.

Thank you that I can trust you.

I know there are other days that are difficult.

Help me to have a heart of goodness

every new day.

And show me how I can bless people around me.

Amen.

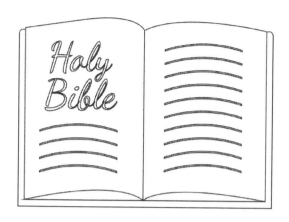

God's Word Says...

"[People] will proclaim the works of God
and ponder what he has done.
The righteous will rejoice in the Lord
and take refuge in him;
all the upright in heart will glory in him!"

Psalm 64:9-10

When You Accomplished Something Good

Lord, thank you for helping me finish. I am glad to sense your love now. I am glad to think of you smiling, Lord Jesus. You deserve credit for every good thing I accomplish. Show me how I can use whatever abilities you have given me, for your glory.

Amen.

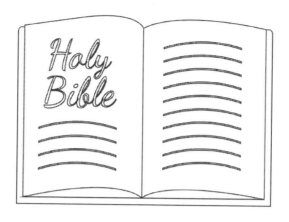

God's Word Says...

"The Lord is good to all;

he has compassion on all he has made.

All your works praise you, Lord;

your faithful people extol you.

They tell of the glory of your kingdom

and speak of your might,

so that all people may know of your mighty acts

and the glorious splendor of your kingdom."

Psalm 145:9-12

(Can you think of something to draw or color here?)

Part 4

Prayers

for
Family
and

Friends

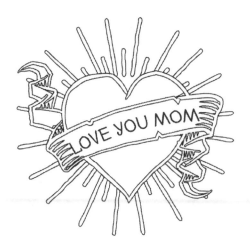

Thanks for Your Mother

Lord, thank you for my mother.

Thank you for the ways she has taken care of me.

Please help her know how much you love her.

Help her on days when she has so much to

accomplish or has a lot of stress.

In Jesus' name, Amen.

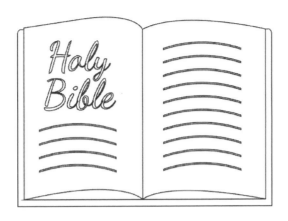

God's Word says...

"Her children arise and call her blessed....

Honor her for all that her hands have done,

and let her works bring her praise."

Proverbs 31:28, 31

_____

(Draw a picture or add your own prayer here.)

Thanks for Your Father

Thank you, God, for my father.

Thank you for the ways he has helped me.

Help him when he has heavy responsibilities to

be able to complete them.

Guide him with your love.

In Jesus' name, Amen.

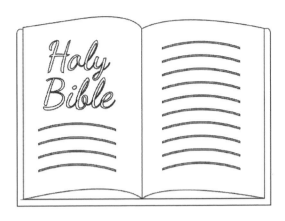

God's Word says...

"As a father has compassion on his children,

so the Lord has compassion on those who fear him."

Psalm 103:13

———————

(Draw a picture or add your own prayer here.)

Thanks for Your Family

I thank you, Lord, for my family.

We are all so different from each other,

and have such different needs,

but I am glad you allow us

to go through life together.

Please help us to support each other.

Help us to know when one of us is hurting.

May our faith be strong.

Amen.

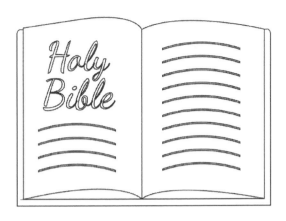

God's Word says...

"For this reason I kneel before the Father, from whom every family in heaven and on earth derives its name."

Ephesians 3:14-15

———————

(Maybe this is a prayer to pray in a special place in your house.)

When Your Father Is Not Doing Well

Lord, please help my father right now.

He really needs you. I know he is strong, but like

anyone else, he can be weak or angry as well.

He is dealing with serious stuff right now.

Help him to find the help he needs.

Show him that he can really trust you.

Help me to be brave and patient while I wait for

things to get better. Amen.

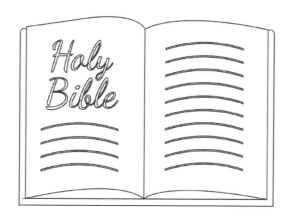

God's Word says...

"Then Jesus told his disciples a parable to show them that they should always pray and not give up."

Luke 18:1

When Your Mother Is Not Doing Well

Lord, I love my mom, and I know she really

needs you right now. These are difficult days.

But I know that things never stay the same.

Help her to hold on to you in faith.

Help her to make good decisions.

Bring alongside her good people who can help.

Give me faith while I wait for things to get better.

In the name of Jesus, Amen.

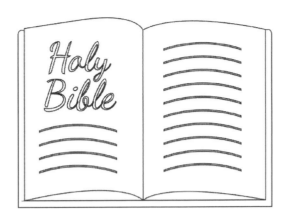

God's Word says...

"I am the Lord your God
*   who takes hold of your right hand*
and says to you, Do not fear;
*   I will help you."*

Psalm 41:13

When Your Friend Is Not Doing Well

Lord, please help my friend.

You know _____ better than I do.

You know what is bothering _____.

I know you love _____.

Please bring your comfort and protection.

Please help _____ to sense your love.

Help me know how to be the best friend

I can be right now. Amen.

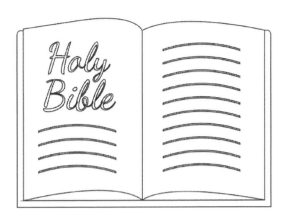

God's Word Says...

"Carry each other's burdens, and in this way you will fulfill the law of Christ."

Galatians 6:2

When Someone You Love Is Ill

I am sad, Lord, because someone I love is very ill.
I wish I could make things better, but I know it is
outside of my control. Please bring good doctors.
Please help everyone make good decisions.
Help me to see how I can be an encouragement.
In Jesus' name, Amen.

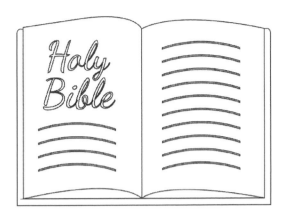

God's Word says...

"So do not fear, for I am with you;
do not be dismayed, for I am your God.
I will strengthen you and help you;
I will uphold you with my righteous right hand."

Isaiah 41:10

For Your School

Lord God, please bless my school, its teachers

and staff, and bless me as I try to do well.

Some times are easy and some times are difficult.

I pray for your help as I study.

I pray for your help as I try to get along with

other students and teachers.

I pray for those who are struggling right now.

I know that you are present everywhere. Help me

to know your presence in every class in every day.

Amen.

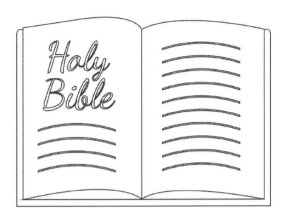

God's Word says...

"I urge you, first of all, to pray for all people. Ask God to help them; intercede on their behalf, and give thanks for them. Pray this way for kings and all who are in authority so that we can live peaceful and quiet lives marked by godliness and dignity. This is good and pleases God our Savior..."

1 Timothy 2:1-3 (TEV)

(Can you think of something to draw or color here?)

Part 5

Prayers for Important Days

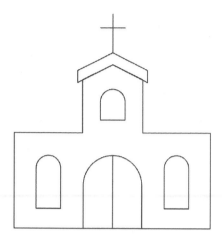

Before Going to Church

Lord, we will soon be going to church.

I want this to help me be closer to you.

Thank you that I can worship and learn.

Thank you that your family includes people all

around the world, and I get to be part of that.

Help me to seek you every day of the week,

wherever I am, and whatever I am doing.

Amen.

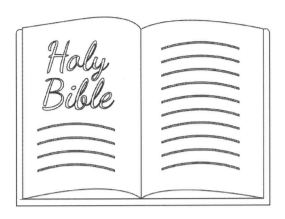

God's Word says...

"Yet a time is coming and has now come when the true worshipers will worship the Father in the Spirit and in truth, for they are the kind of worshipers the Father seeks."

John 4:23

On Your Birthday

Thank you, Lord,

for your blessings in my life in the last year.

I do not know what I will face in the year ahead.

I know there will be good things,

and there will be difficult things.

I pray that you will help me live a good and

honorable life.

In Jesus' name, Amen.

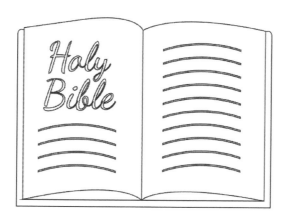

God's Word Says...

"For we are God's handiwork, created in Christ Jesus to do good works, which God prepared in advance for us to do."

Ephesians 2:10

For the Beginning of the School Year

Lord, please bless these first days of class this
year. I know I have to adjust to many new things.
So help me to understand, help me to have a
good start with teachers,
and old friends, and new friends.
I believe I will learn new things this year that will
help me grow and prepare me for life.
Amen.

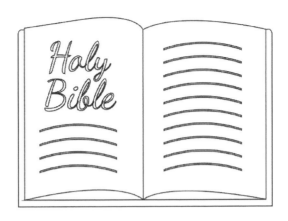

God's Word says...

"Trust in the Lord with all your heart

and lean not on your own understanding;

in all your ways submit to him,

and he will make your paths straight."

Proverbs 3:5-6

For the End of the School Year

Thank you, Lord, that I have been able to finish
another year of school.
Please take the seeds of what I have learned
and grow them in my life.
Help me to understand what I have learned
through difficulties this year.
Thank you now for this break from school.
I remain your student at all times, Teacher Jesus.
I am listening.
Amen.

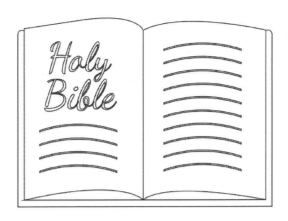

God's Word says...

"Therefore everyone who hears these words of mine and puts them into practice is like a wise man who built his house on the rock. The rain came down, the streams rose, and the winds blew and beat against that house; yet it did not fall, because it had its foundation on the rock. But everyone who hears these words of mine and does not put them into practice is like a foolish man who built his house on sand. The rain came down, the streams rose, and the winds blew and beat against that house, and it fell with a great crash."

Matthew 7:24-27

At Christmas Time

Lord God, thank you that you so loved all of us

that you sent your only Son to forgive us.

We celebrate Jesus' birth in Bethlehem.

Now we know you are with us.

We know we are forgiven.

We know you will correct all the evil in the world.

I am glad to get gifts for Christmas, but you, Lord

Jesus, are the greatest gift.

Help me to give good things to others. Amen.

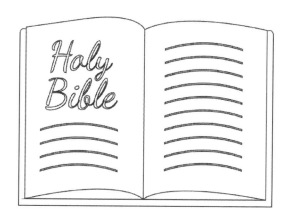

God's Word says...

"For to us a child is born,

to us a son is given,

and the government will be on his shoulders.

And he will be called

Wonderful Counselor, Mighty God,

Everlasting Father, Prince of Peace.

Of the greatness of his government and peace

there will be no end."

Isaiah 9:6-7

At Easter Time

Dear God, I believe in the Lord Jesus…

who was born in Bethlehem, who grew up and

became a man, who taught crowds of people, who

loved his disciples, who healed the sick, who was

arrested by his enemies, was called a criminal, was

nailed to a cross.

He died and was placed in a tomb; but on the

third day, he rose.

I believe I am forgiven because of Jesus.

And I believe I can be strong because he is alive

and is with me today. Amen.

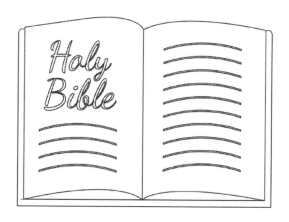

God's Word Says...

I want to know Christ—yes, to know the power of his resurrection and participation in his sufferings, becoming like him in his death, and so, somehow, attaining to the resurrection from the dead."

Philippians 3:10-11

The Prayer Jesus Taught

Our Father in heaven,

hallowed be your name,

your kingdom come,

your will be done,

on earth as it is in heaven.

Give us today our daily bread.

And forgive us our debts,

as we also have forgiven our debtors.

And lead us not into temptation,

but deliver us from the evil one.

Matthew 6:9-13

One-Sentence Prayers

- Thank you, Jesus.
- I really need you now, dear God.
- You are stronger, Lord,
  than anyone who picks on me.
- Help my family, oh Lord.
- I am sorry for what I said, Lord.
- Give me the right words to say, dear God.
- Please help [*name of family member*] today.
- Keep us safe as we travel, dear Lord.
- Dear God, give me courage today.
- Help Mom and Dad today, dear Lord.
- Dear God, I praise you for your goodness.

My Prayers

My Prayers

Do you ever wish you understood the Bible better?

Almost everyone does. Mature believers and new believers. Young and old. Those who have read the Bible for years and those just starting out.

How to Understand the Bible: A Simple Guide, will help you gain an overall perspective on the flow and meaning of Scripture. It addresses questions like: What is the big picture of the Bible? What about Bible translations? How should we understand the stories of the Old Testament? How should we interpret what the prophets had to say? How should we understand the teachings of Jesus? What was Jesus teaching in the parables? How can we hear God's voice in Scripture? What are the proper ways to apply Scripture to life today?

www.WordWay.org

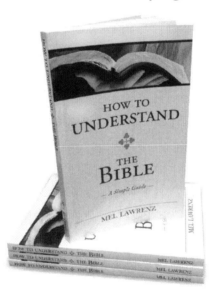

Made in the USA
Lexington, KY
24 April 2019